EVERYWHERE AT ONCE

For Brendan,

Another Just Man,
+ my favorite golf
buddy,

Love, William, ysu,
'08

AKRON SERIES IN POETRY

Akron Series in Poetry

Mary Biddinger, Editor

Barry Seiler, *The Waters of Forgetting*
Raeburn Miller, *The Comma After Love:*
  Selected Poems of Raeburn Miller
William Greenway, *How the Dead Bury the Dead*
Jon Davis, *Scrimmage of Appetite*
Anita Feng, *Internal Strategies*
Susan Yuzna, *Her Slender Dress*
Raeburn Miller, *The Collected Poems of Raeburn Miller*
Clare Rossini, *Winter Morning with Crow*
Barry Seiler, *Black Leaf*
William Greenway, *Simmer Dim*
Jeanne E. Clark, *Ohio Blue Tips*
Beckian Fritz Goldberg, *Never Be the Horse*
Marlys West, *Notes for a Late-Blooming Martyr*
Dennis Hinrichsen, *Detail from* The Garden of Earthly Delights
Susan Yuzna, *Pale Bird, Spouting Fire*
John Minczeski, *Circle Routes*
Barry Seiler, *Frozen Falls*
Elton Glaser and William Greenway, eds.,
  I Have My Own Song for It: Modern Poems of Ohio
Melody Lacina, *Private Hunger*
George Bilgere, *The Good Kiss*
William Greenway, *Ascending Order*
Roger Mitchell, *Delicate Bait*
Lynn Powell, *The Zones of Paradise*
Dennis Hinrichsen, *Cage of Water*
Sharmila Voorakkara, *Fire Wheel*
Kurt Brown, Meg Kearney, Donna Reis, Estha Weiner, eds.,
  Blues for Bill: A Tribute to William Matthews
Vern Rutsala, *How We Spent Our Time*
Clare Rossini, *Lingo*
Beckian Fritz Goldberg, *The Book of Accident*
Ashley Capps, *Mistaking the Sea for Green Fields*
Roger Mitchell, *Half/Mask*
Alison Pelegrin, *Big Muddy River of Stars*
Jeff Gundy, *Spoken among the Trees*
Brian Brodeur, *Other Latitudes*
William Greenway, *Everywhere at Once*

EVERYWHERE

AT

ONCE

WILLIAM GREENWAY

The University of Akron Press
Akron, Ohio

11 10 09 08 07 5 4 3 2 1

Library of Congress Cataloging-in-Publication Data
Greenway, William, 1947–
Everywhere at once / William Greenway.
     p. cm. — (Akron series in poetry)
Includes bibliographical references and index.
ISBN 978-1-931968-56-0 (pbk. : alk. paper)
I. Title.
PS3557.R3969E94 2008
811'.54—dc22
                              2008024053
The paper used in this publication meets the minimum requirements of American National Standard for Information Sciences—Permanence of Paper for Printed Library Materials, ANSI Z39.48–1984. ∞

Acknowledgments
88: A Journal of Contemporary American Poetry, "Praying"; *America*, "The Audition"; *Artful Dodge*, "Just Man," "Shinto"; *Atlanta Review*, "Orpheus and the Ex-Mrs. Lot"; *Basalt*, "O'Sisyphus Tours," "The Path to Iskeroon," "The Dead Use Us for Their Pleasure"; *Bryant Literary Review*, "The Interpretation of Dreams"; *Cave Wall*, "Twm Siôn Cati's Cave"; *Ekphrasis*, "Fishing for Souls"; *Front Range Review*, "~~Mediation, Medication,~~ Meditation," "The Husband, Upon the Wife's Returning Home"; *Hurricane Blues: Poems about Katrina and Rita* (Southeast Missouri State University Press, 2006), "Storm Surge"; *In a Fine Frenzy: Poets Respond to Shakespeare* (University of Iowa Press, 2005), "Ophelia Writes Home"; *The Laurel Review*, "Tenebrae"; *The Ledge Magazine*, "Three Stories"; *Louisiana Literature*, "Holding on to the Pommel," "The Keys of Women," "Portrait of the Artist as a Young Boy"; *Mississippi Review*, "Hutch," "Ophelia Writes Home"; *Planet: The Welsh Internationalist*, "Battle of the Bulge"; Poetry Daily, "Orpheus and the Ex-Mrs. Lot"; *Poetry Wales*, "Gross Anatomy" (as "The Autopsy Poems"); *Prairie Schooner*, "Perseverance"; *Rhino*, "Applesauce"; *Shenandoah*, "Spot On"; *Southern Poetry Review*, "Why We Never Had Kids"; *The Southern Review*, "Canterbury Tale," "Parallel Man," "The Side to the Wall"; *The Spoon River Poetry Review*, "Persephone" (as "Eurydice"); *Tar Wolf Review*, "St. David's Day"; *Toledo Review*, "The Unusual Suspects"; *Twice Removed* (Main Street Rag's Editor's Choice Chapbook Series, 2006), "Erratum," "Mary Morgans," "Otherworld," "Parallel Man," "Red Sky at Morning," "The Wolves of Wales," "The Others," "Two Minds," "Forensics," "Fishing for Souls," "Elect," "Roman Holiday," "The Path to Iskeroon," "The Dead Use Us for Their Pleasure," "Portsmouth," "Directions," "Our Lady of No Layovers," "O'Sisyphus Tours," "Hounds of Heaven," "The Place You Belong," "The Interpretation of Dreams," "Twice Removed."

I thank Youngstown State University for the sabbatical that enabled me to write this book.

Cover: *Umbrellas* (1927), Antonio Petruccelli. Used by permission.

Contents

I. Assisted Living
Everywhere at Once   3
Portrait of the Artist as a Young Boy   4
Bump   5
Ophelia Writes Home   7
Shinto   8
Perseverance   9
The Audition   10
The Olympus Food Court   11
Feeding Time at The Fuel and Fuddle   12
Assisted Living   13
Battle of the Bulge   14
Orpheus and the Ex-Mrs. Lot: A Second Marriage   15
The Side to the Wall   17
Just Man   18
The Keys of Women   20
Play, for the Night Is Coming   21
Gross Anatomy   23
The Crash   25
The Loaves and Fishes   26
The Husband, Upon the Wife's Returning Home   27
~~Mediation~~, ~~Medication~~, Meditation   29
The Unusual Suspects   30
Bogeyman   31
Late   33

II. Twice Removed

Erratum   37

Mary Morgans   38

Otherworld   40

Parallel Man   41

Red Sky at Morning   42

The Wolves of Wales   43

The Others   44

Two Minds   45

Forensics   46

Fishing for Souls   47

Elect   49

Roman Holiday   51

The Path to Iskeroon   53

The Dead Use Us for Their Pleasure   54

Portsmouth   55

Directions   57

Our Lady of No Layovers   58

O'Sisyphus Tours   60

Holding on to the Pommel   61

The Place You Belong   62

Hounds of Heaven   63

The Interpretation of Dreams   65

Twice Removed   66

III. Storm Surge

Persephone   71

The Night Before We Left   72

Cells   73

The Hard of Hearing   74

Long Love Sonnet   75

The Angel in the Elevator   76

Smackdown   78

Praying   80

Hutch   81

St. David's Day   82

Spot On   83

Three Stories   84

Why We Never Had Kids   85

Once, Driving in England, in Winter, in Rain   86

Twm Siôn Cati's Cave   87

Tenebrae   88

Applesauce   89

Honey   90

Canterbury Tale   91

Storm Surge   92

For Betty, for her bravery

I

ASSISTED

LIVING

Everywhere at Once

Even in Kyoto,
Hearing the cuckoo's cry,
I long for Kyoto.
—Basho

Why does my brain always suddenly
flash to the places I've been in France or Italy,
and mostly Wales, when I'm only
boiling an egg or putting on my shoes,
which are neither French nor Italian
and especially not Welsh? I've even dream-
traveled to places I've never been, like
palmy Papeete or balmy Bali, or
India, where I swear I used to live, a boy
whipping the flanks of a water buffalo
on the banks of a red dust river like
the Chattahoochee, where I was reared
this time around. I should be a Hindu
instead of a Southern Baptist preacher's kid
gone south, the way I space-time trip
to the triple play of Atlanta, New Orleans,
Portland. Once by the Irish Sea,
I couldn't even see it, so blinded
was I by the lean of my yearn
for Sanibel Island, Florida. But this
is the whirling compass, the bong
and ping of the psychic pinball
of karma, and with the world cocked
at twenty-three degrees, what else can we do
but tilt?

Portrait of the Artist
as a Young Boy

I drove my big sister nuts
as she tried to sleep in our shared bedroom
while I crooned to the dark "America
the Beautiful" or "The Marines' Hymn."
"Get him out!" she'd cry to my mother.
"He's so weird!"
So Mother tried reading to me,
stories, poems, and I'd sleep,
until the night she read Field's
"Little Boy Blue," how the toy
soldier waited staunchly in
the attic for the little boy who died
to come back and play with him.
I cried so long and hard, she finally
had to put me in a cold bath
and give me hiccups.
After that, I made up my own songs,
my sister weeping every night as I sang
of a little toy soldier who ran
in the amber heaven of waves
of grain, or waited forever
in the hell of the empty halls
of Monty Zooma, or on the desolate
shores of Triple Lee.

Bump

It appears that some of my cells have opted
for quixotic careers of their own.
                    —William Gibson

The readiness is all.
                    —Hamlet

It's been a week now since he sliced it
from my nose, and I await the verdict.
Death is a fearful thing, says my
Shakespeare calendar for today,
though maybe not as bad as a future
scurrying from the shadows of alleys
with a tin cup, or life beneath a tent
as The Hideous Noseless Man, who looks
a lot like the skeletal, acid-melted, phantom
face of Lon Chaney.

Auden, when someone died
of throat cancer, said, *It's because*
he was a liar. I wonder if my *o'ergrowth*
of complexion is from sticking it in
where it doesn't belong, or if brown-
nosing is my *vicious mole of nature*.
Or perhaps this time I'll just get a warning.
In Britain, they call a speed bump, that
hump of asphalt like a mound
of new grave, a sleeping policeman, blue
body prone in the road, arms

straight at his sides, eyes closed,
as if to ask, *And where do you
think you're going in such
a hurry, Squire?* Reminding me
how fast I was headed for the hairpin
turn of my unreadiness.

Ophelia Writes Home

He passed so peacefully in sleep, it seemed
as in a kingly way, or in at least
what passes for a royal death in this
rough place where every bush may hide a bear.
He was a good provider, and we lived
if not as kings, then as two princes who
were born to make the best of baser things
and not forget how blessed we were to be
alive at all. It was Horatio,
you now can know, who hatched the plan to bate
the sword with sleeping potion, culled from stuff
he'd read at school in Wittenberg about
the young Italian lovers, feuding tribes,
a tomb for two. It just remained to bribe
the graveyard clowns to feign and shuttle both
the boxes (I no longer shivering
and wet) on board the pirate ship we dubbed
The Nunnery, a little jest which fed
the joy we felt in one another's arms
across the icy sea, until we reached
this Eden Danish men discovered past
the coldest land of all. Our children grew,
the crops rose tall, the swarthy neighbors brought
their harvest in to honor us at fall.
This is in secret—should you draw your breath
to tell his tale do not this letter show,
thereby his famous tragedy amending.
Recall his melancholy cast and know
how much he would abhor a happy ending.

Shinto

I sort of like the idea of our ancestors
looking after us from some kind of heaven,
though I hope they're not watching all the time,
or if they are, they see only pixilated parts
like the faces of alleged criminals
and full-frontals of horny youngsters
on reality shows. I've always had guardian
angels, of course, but generic, before anybody
I love had died. And we all need backup,
officer down, the blue lights of halos
wailing toward my next accident or assault
or even intervening before I step out
absent-mindedly into a busy street.
They'd flash their badges of silver wings,
the traffic squalling to a hot rubber halt,
while my disappointed mother, now
wearing gloves as white as doves,
waves me across.

Perseverance

My mother used to wear out belts
on my bony body, once broke
a Ouija board over my head,
and Daddy would sermonize till the cows
covered their ears, doctrine
off a duck's back. Schools only gave me
degrees to get me out, and girls got
so tired of saying *no* that they married me.
Maybe perversity grows from a gene,
like grass through a sidewalk,
or hardens and mottles like a shell around
some soft psychic tissue till you have
an organ that plods on while the hares
are sleeping. And so as soon as Mother
would forbid me to go to the creek,
the dogs and I headed there like newts.
And when I finally went too far
that summer at the beach,
and the lifeguard had to bring me back in
to another whipping, I just kept grinning
at how far I'd gotten,
how many waves I'd broken
with my hard head.

The Audition

In this game, we confess the things
about ourselves we've never told
before: Gary wearing the same shirt
for all four of his high school class pictures,
Jim doing something slightly shady
for the CIA in Nam, Kelly dancing topless
that summer to get through grad school.
I hesitate between the public swimming pool
when I was ten, or sitting on my brother's face
and breaking his nose, till I remember
Terry Mayo, not only the prettiest girl
in first grade, but maybe ever, so lovely
she was born for Frank Harris, who wore
a coat and tie to school and, even I could see,
was handsome as a movie star. A little
sheepishly, I decide to scrawl on my scrap
of paper how, for her birthday, I gave her
a brown-plastic-framed picture
of Jesus, knowing my friends will laugh
for years to come. But what they won't know
is how she suddenly kissed me bang
on the mouth in the middle of the playground
in front of God and everybody, or that, when
Christmas came, it was not me, but Frank, gold
in the robe his mother made, who knelt
in the straw with the sheep, while I stood
next to her, cotton wool on my chin,
towel on my head, and felt
with my hand, for a full ten minutes,
her waist, tiny and warm.

The Olympus Food Court

From my table by plate glass,
I look past the toothbrush bristles
of spruce toward Mt. Hood, extinct
volcano, sugared with snow, and St.
Helens that blew its spire, though still
higher than I am now.
Below me, the high-heeled,
short-skirted nymph makes for
her blood-red convertible in only
a clingy knit top, nipples fronting
the wind, facing down the season,
and I long to lose this low-cal
salad, descend, and chase her
as satyr, centaur, stag.

But that was B.C. or B.C.E. or whatever
the hell embarrassed initials
they give that golden age,
and my jogging-suited, running-shoed,
blue-haired, bejeweled wife returns
with the consolation of frozen yogurt
to yank me back from boardom
into boredom, old goat
chewing his memory cud
of ambrosial girls and the silver
platter of that world where I fed
on pink confections of horizon
and the high fat of the flesh.

Feeding Time at The Fuel and Fuddle

I come here to batten on the blood
of the young, the brick walls
deafening with all their burble
of babble, hormones thick in the air
as grill grease and cigarette smoke.
Already they're raring to make
their first mistakes, the ones
they'll have to live with like monogamy
long as this mahogany bar.
Immune to calories, they
pound down pizza, fries, tuns
of local beers, thinking their whippet
waistlines will last forever, even longer
than their livers. I,
invisible as a gray ghost,
order a third martini, effete
drink for so yeasty and lusty,
hoppy and happy a crowd
fermenting in its own imagined future.
I order a rare ribeye: "Just knock
the horns off and run it out,"
I smirk to the pert young waitress,
and when she does, say, "I've seen
cows burnt worse than this get well."
She smiles and shies away, though
I've forgotten to ask for my wine,
a sturdy, old-growth zin,
full-bodied with a touch of tartness
and a bite of bramble.

Assisted Living

I walk the long carpeted hall past Norman Rockwell prints
and gray doors with dried flowers and cards
slipped into bronze frames, bearing their
shaky-handed names, the names
of their time: Ethel, Bertha, Elsie,
Bessie, the Mildred all the boys
wanted to marry, Frances, the great dancer,
and Florence with her good, full figure.
Mary was still the most popular
name into the fifties, but now
has fallen to fiftieth on the list.
Hard to believe someday
the cards will read Sierra, Kylie,
Courtney, their blue rose and butterfly
tattoos wrinkled and shrunken
like the faces on burst balloons,
their husbands, Tyler, Cody, Ryan,
in the ground twenty years now,
flesh still steeped in alcohol,
nicotine, cholesterol,
hands coupled
above their ruptured hearts.

Battle of the Bulge

Because he almost froze, hunkered
in snowy trenches beneath a sky
too clotted for air support,
and because the padres prayed
for a clear Christmas day
so we could bomb the Germans and win
the battle, then the war, he still believes
in prayer, how it can veer the smoke
of his leaf-fire away from his house
to drift and fuddle the pines
of his pagan neighbors across the lake,
and how the hurricane can be coaxed
to punish the godless casinos
of the panhandle.
And who's to say different?
(Tokyo was cloudy, Hiroshima clear.)
My own father once said, "Of course
you can bargain with God," trade one thing
for another, the *quid pro quo* of the cross.
And so I, too, still dicker with the deity,
especially when pinned down, surrounded
like the Seventh Army by gluttony, greed,
lust, pride, etcetera, that, when pressed
down here, always bulges up there,
an inner tube of spirit in heavy water.
Yes, I do pray the skies uncloud,
the air turn blue and clear above
the head of this atheist
stuck in another foxhole, waiting
for squadrons of angels to swoop down
and drop on all my darknesses
their payloads of light.

Orpheus and the Ex-Mrs. Lot:
A Second Marriage

It's been a hell of a time,
too much alike in too many ways,
me still writing poems to dead parents
and old wives, and you back down
south with your fundamentalist father
who claims to be dying again, weeping
so hard on the phone every night
I'm afraid that bulge of blood
in your brain might finally burst,
or that your tears will turn you
to salt, and nothing I sing
or say can help—he won't read
or even hear how much
I need you up here. His head
is cocked on the pillow, listening
to his boombox hymns
and making you listen, too.

Let the dead bury the dead,
come home again,
and let's start over,
rewrite the myths to get us
beyond all this,
so when you see me
up the long hallway
from the gate

and my face appears
to be turned away
toward the terminal,
don't doubt this time,
just follow.
I won't look back
if you won't.

The Side to the Wall

Considering this is the last Christmas tree
in Hattiesburg, Mississippi, it's not bad.
I recall all of the childhood lots, white
breath on the night air as gloved, rough men
held trees by the horns like trophies, stabbing
the stobs into the ground to show
how the needles, still fresh, stuck,
arguing the limbs would loosen, spread
like wings when left alone, given a good home.

But always the ribs of one side
stayed stove in from where it lay,
or were scraggled being dragged
from underneath the others.
We turned it to the wall, stinting
the lights and tinsel so as not to call
attention. Those limbs lived in shadow,
like the black of the moon, out
of reach, ungarnished, ungraced,
holding their dark like a slice of night,
below the awful angel that turned
its back and faced the light.

Just Man

Then Joseph her husband, being a just man,
and not willing to make her a public example,
was minded to put her away privately.
—Matthew 1:19

Having a famous father-in-law
never helped him much, hurt,
really, the way his wife kowtowed:
His will be done.
And the story of the angel in the garden
must have been hard to swallow,
though he hoped his faith would
make him a savior in her eyes.
Instead, he was squeezed out first
of a honeymoon hotel, then
a barn by kneeling oxen, the stench
of shepherds, and strangers wearing turbans.
The gold was great, yes, but what
could you do with frankincense,
and what the hell was myrrh?
Admittedly, the child turned out
better than expected, never even cried,
even looked a little like him, happy
for hours playing in the sawdust pile.
But then, of course, everything went wrong
at the end, and she mourned so much
she never came to him again.
Still, he must have told himself, you don't
have to be happy, there's no *requirement,*

and so he learned the contentment
of the ordinary—sunrise, steam
of breakfast, smell of shavings and sweat
in the shop—the satisfaction
of doing small things well, sawing
studs, sanding the rough grain smooth,
nailing one piece of wood
across another.

The Keys of Women

Men and women are two locked caskets,
each of which contains the key to the other.
—Isak Dinesen

Maybe it's Freud, maybe just because
they have no pockets, those linty
scrotums, that they must carry them
cupped in their palms till they're lost
or again mislaid among the bric-a-brac.
Men know exactly where they are,
always, feel the steely stabs in the thigh,
the tearing at the seam, carting all
they think will unlock whatever's barred,
perhaps even women themselves, those
rummagers in purses for combs and cosmetics—
their own hinges and hasps—hoping
somehow to finally lose what
someone else might find and share:
the key to the dark stair
down to all they've locked away
but forgotten where.

Play, for the Night Is Coming

The corkboard in the dark, chill vestibule
of the eleventh-century Norman church
announces: "THE SERVICE WILL BE
GIN AT 5 O'CLOCK." And will be
every night, praise God,
world without end.

Our Southern Baptist church
was no cathedral, the only light
fluorescent, no bleeding statues
nor black-lacquered Bible scenes,
just the watery watercolor
of the River Jordan on the wall
behind the baptistery
where I was dunked at seven,
and Jesus suffered brown and yellow children
under date palms in the nursery.
Our shot-glass blood was Welch's grape,
His body broken in saltines
on burgundy velvet in
the silver-plated plates.
We kids took the biggest shards
since the squirming sermons dragged
away past noon. Once, I heard
Preacher Daniel's "Let us pray,"
as a dozy "play," impossible
since this was Sunday.

But now it's time to stop this reminiscence—
the sun is over the yard-arm of the cross at, what?
the sixteenth hour? Bringing in the sheaves,

if only of paper and memory, is thirsty work.
The slanting gold of afternoon
through high windows rivals the tall
and garish panes of Chartres,
and pierces like a spear of light the font
of my martini glass. It's time for Nones,
Vespers, whatever, and now I hold my own
high, mixed-up mass, stick the thorn
of toothpick in a skull of olive,
dip it, lick the chrism
from its little, briny brow,
and eat the host, immortal now.

Gross Anatomy

—after judging a poetry contest for medical students

It is difficult
to get the news from poems
yet men die miserably every day
for lack
of what is found there.
                    —William Carlos Williams

Half their poems are sick from watching,
for the first time, someone die, pale
and helpless amid the drone and drip

of machines, and the rest suffer
the thing itself, the empty hands, blue
as Dührer's, into which they place again,

in their minds and on paper, the toys,
roses, and other hands they once held.
But though they saw open the skull,

raise the pate on its waste-bin hinge,
lift out the brain, and stare into the bowl
where they imagine memories still float

like petals on dark water, and though they
"crack" the chest with a melon sound, lift
and weigh the liver and lights, and hold

in their hands the heavy heart,
it's the shrunken sex and withered breasts
that prove too much for ones so young,

and impel them to try and tell, witness
to what they have seen. And so they write
it down, send it off, then wait to hear

that it has won, for how can it miss
since it really happened, even the names—
embolism, arteriovenus, curettage—pure poetry.

The Crash

Another week in a hell
of disks, droning reboots, re-
loading, rebooting, as if my vicious
circle were in the inferno.
My ear forms to the phone
as another voice like Gandhi's
tries to lead me out of the labyrinth,
though, as we're told, the way out
is the way through, past the puzzle
wrapping the enigma, into the mystery,
then burrowing down to a page of code,
like delving beneath the derma
to alter the DNA,
or going even deeper to read
a Rosetta Stone of the subatomic level.

But nothing ever works,
and we start again, still broken and alone,
the world beyond the windows dwindling
to the Weather Channel, leaving
just the blue porthole to peer through
at the strange and glowing forms
of the seafloor, a life away and twenty
thousand leagues below the light,
like those Russian sailors, their sub
sinking in the silt, waiting for either salvation
or implosion, nothing left to breathe
but their own breath.

The Loaves and Fishes

is a bar outside of Bethlehem,
PA, where once your gin glass is filled,
it stays filled, like the clear, inexhaustible stuff
of the cosmos, and every swig begins
another big bang. Even the vermouth
grows from a single dewdrop and swirls
into another solar system, matter
never being destroyed, only . . . etcetera, etcetera.
So many universes down the smoky bar,
each held by its own little drunken deity,
who quaffs and holds forth on the meaning
of things, hoping the prophets
of the new olive-green planets
are taking all of this down.

The Husband, Upon the Wife's Returning Home

It seems like only yesterday the tanker truck
backed up to the house and hosed
its bourbon into the basement,

and I woke to the castanets of cassettes
on the porch as the porn man made
his rounds. The future seemed to stretch

in amber haze to the sky, and the sun
rose red as a fried egg dappled with Tabasco
or the microwave bubbling of barbecued wings.

What fun we had, fellas, I say
to the furniture layered in clothes
as if they've been to a Packers game,

but now we have the Herculean
task of putting everything back
exactly as it was, though I can't

remember where you were stationed,
wearing your dress blues before we stood
down and unbuttoned.

And what cultures have clabbered
in the petri dishes of the sink, what dis-
eases spread in cankers

on the laces and linen? Perhaps
some deep, demonic *déshabillé*
seduced me to stray into this shabby

sin that wrenched her house awry,
and I just a weak-minded faller-in
with bad companions, or at least

that's what this penitent will plead,
and she, being flesh, will certainly relent,
knowing how I can't be sent away

to rehab, be repainted, reupholstered.
She never trusted me anyway, maybe
even left to prove what she already knew—

all my petty weaknesses, how
with even the smallest of excuses I
fell so readily into pieces, sank

into sloth and everything the mother
warns the bride against—a life
like dirty socks, mismatched and unmended.

~~Mediation~~, ~~Medication~~, Meditation

It's drunk and I'm late, but
I worry I should write down something
for prosperity—something
sage, which is an herb (notice
the cultured "an" and the aspirated "h"),
for poesy should be at least
instructional if not constructional, no?
For where in the world would we be if not
for the unacknowledged legislation
some bastard always filibusters:
(I yield the floor to the Congressman
from Martini and his aginda.)
And yet, and yet, perhaps
there's something left to be said.
We can't all go as mute as swans
just because everything's been written.
If I repeat yourself, very well,
I repeat yourself. You're vast, you contain
multitudes. In fact, what an excellent
reader you are! What's your name anyway?
No matter—you're The Reader, and it's enough
I feel you snuggling my neck as you lean
out of the smug window of the future to read
over my shoulder, which you pat to say,
Go to bed now; sleep.
Whatever you have omitted or forgotten
will still be there in the morning.

The Unusual Suspects

"*Round up the usual suspects.*"
—Captain Louis Renault, *Casablanca*

I suppose these would be people like us,
who've never done anything "wrong," whose
portraits never hung in the post office gallery.
We're furtive, yes, but not like that nice
young/old man who turns out to be
a cannibal or paedophile,
just the sort who uses ae instead of an e
and simpers about wines. While
the usual suspects distract
the authorities, we fritter away
at all kinds of filth—filching from
the office, being poetic without license,
dreaming adulteries (and while awake!),
driving in open containers under the influence
of radio rock or Updike novels on tape,
committing gross indemnity, or
impersonating a police philosopher.
If only we'd had an indecent upbringing,
not fallen in with bland companions,
we, too, might have made nothing
of our lives, become most wanted, armed
and dangerous, instead of disarming,
smug, small-time, and still at large.

Bogeyman

Whose woods these are, I think I know …

I shall be telling this with a sigh
Somewhere ages and ages hence.

Nobody would play with me today,
so I went by myself. Though it's the peak
of the turning leaves, the course
is empty. Who
needs other people anyway?
I was born naked, says Dr. Williams.
I am better so.

At such times I hit two balls
and take the best. Dr. Jekyll
always pars while Mr. Hyde
wanders in the woods
and into my boyhood, all
those afternoons in goldengrove,
dreaming of women,
smelling those leaves like sex
and death at once.

The bees think my ball's a late flower,
and it is getting late, the shadows rising.
Let night come. How bad
could it be? A few
hollow pumpkins, some skeletons
and bedsheets, a Hyde or two.

Lost one Halloween, caught
by the dark, I found
my way home, scaring the monsters
and ghosts by blowing the disc
from the broken belly
of a doll.
Ma ma, ma ma, the trees heard,
and the owls answered *who, who,*
and my steps in the fallen leaves
whispered their decay,
this way, this way.

Late

We were never on time for anything,
though Daddy rattled the car keys in the hall
while Mother puffed her hair another inch.
We even missed the seasons,
got to the mountains too late
for autumn colors, looked instead
at bare trees and walked on dead leaves
brown as cracklings. Only their deaths
were early, and they were right on time
for those. I'm left alone, and feel
like the gray mule we saw that winter day,
going round and round in the old way,
grinding the cane that was, though late,
still sweet.

II

TWICE
REMOVED

Erratum

"Live from Whales"
—caption on the ABC Evening News

Seen from space, it's the head
of a boar, and we lived on a tusk
slavered with the Severn Sea,
camped blowy nights
on the snout snuffling
the north Atlantic, one time
had tea with a famous poet
who lived like a flea in a floppy ear.
That quiff on top?
Rhododendrons of the mountains
where Hillary trained.
Within that flinty head,
we've driven past
the source of Stonehenge,
through tar-black quarries
that slated half the roofs
of the world. The stones
of the houses are woven
like shawls, and its greenest
of green is always sprinkled
with the salt of sheep
to bring out the savor
of holiday snaps.
Here in *Cymru* my grandfather
and Dylan Thomas were born,
and every hill and chapel
once echoed with poem
and hymn. Wales:
where even the coal mines—
so many mouths of the earth—
welled with praise.

Mary Morgans

Mary Morgans is my name
Wales is my nation
Llanddoisant is my dwelling place
And Christ is my salvation
When I am dead and in my grave
And all my bones are rotten
Inside this frame you will find my name
When I am quite forgotten
                    Born in the year 1847, aged 23

She's bedeviled us ever since we got
to this sixteenth-century stone cowshed,
now a cottage with samplers
on the walls, hers stitched in 1870.
Sometimes, we feel her hovering just
beyond our sight, or as reflections
of garden birds flitting past the windows.
Sometimes, she mists a bit of mirror,
like breath. The VCR eats all my tapes,
the lights and TV go off and on,
the freezer door opens in the middle
of the night and the floor is flooded
by breakfast. The computers crash,
and she plucks at our slippers to trip
us on the steep stairs. She seems
to want dissension between us,
or maybe she's jealous, but of whom?
We fantasize her life, an orphan maid's,
born exactly a hundred years before me,
cut short by one of the floods that sluiced
the valley, leaving no lover or child
behind her. We've combed the local
churchyards and can't find her—

no stone remembers her, though
on our knees in the morning, swabbing,
swabbing our little flood, we sing:
Mary, Mary, quite contrary,
though all your bones are rotten,
you've sewn your name into our lives,
you'll never be forgotten.

Otherworld

*Even the dogs in West Kerry know that the Otherworld
exists and that to be in and out of it constantly is
the most natural thing in the world.*
—Nuala Ní Dhomhnaill

This is where a woman fell
to her death the other day,
climbing the cliff.
They found her face-up, spread-eagled
on the sand, as if she'd been ravished
by a god, or tried to fly.
On this rare hot day in Wales,
hang-gliders fill the Down above,
each aspiring Icarus fluttering
silken, colored wings like the butterflies
in the gorse, which smells, the guidebooks
always say, of "desiccated coconut,"
like the ghost of some tropical isle.
She scaled these strata of seafloor
crowded up into the air until they grew
green and strewn with sheep on top,
where we walk and flirt with the edge
that boys clamber down to fish the ledges.
And though the border collies
bark at azure sea and sky, and try
to herd us back to safety,
as if they hear something we don't
out there, we lean, and listen.

Parallel Man

He comes up behind us so soundlessly
he might have risen from the mist.
We didn't even hear the tire-
crunch of his ancient bicycle on this
gravel path by the cairn of an Ice Age tribe.
Now I know what novels mean by a suit
"shiny with wear" or "threadbare,"
or a shirt "yellowed with time." His tie,
though, is well-knotted, and he's white-
haired, Welsh-small, and almost natty.
Ignoring me, he talks to the boy
of parallel universes: "Oh, they're everywhere,
you know, all around us. They go on and on."
He finally rides off toward the woods,
but when we turn back, he's vanished,
and since no one else has seen him,
the kid is spooked, and I tease him, saying,
it's like he knew you, maybe your Welsh
grandfather born in the village nearby,
come to tell you something.
They're all around here, ghosts, I say,
like the hangman who hanged himself,
or Paviland Man, found in a cave
just over there on the coast, dead
for twenty-six thousand years, his bones
festooned with tigers' saber teeth
and wooly mammoth hair,
daubed with ochre and trinketed,
tricked out to the nines, as if
he were going someplace far away,
or as near as here and now.

Red Sky at Morning

Red sky at morning, sailor take warning;
Red sky at night, sailor's delight!

These old Welsh oaks are having
their hair styled again tonight,
swept to one side like Elvis
impersonators, permed and pomaded
with a gel of North Atlantic sleet.
The sunlit lanes we walked all summer,
and the cliff-top, yellow-flowered gorse
and pink heather bells are getting
a comb-through, too, even the shag
of wild moorland ponies soused
and groomed. A wind so loud
it wakes the dead, who jostle
at the windows of this old stone
barn like a press-gang of ghosts,
weary of icy waves and shipwreck shoals,
just want a nice cuppa, promise
no clanking chains or moans, just gentle
apparitions on the stairs and soft
sentimental old songs on the parlor upright.
But we cower from the doorknocks:
although such vapors rinse the dawn red
and pink the sunset above the bay,
it'll be hell to clean up,
and there'll be heaven to pay.

The Wolves of Wales

Wolves were here in olden days.
The seeing-eye hound of Hervé, blind bard,
was savaged by a wolf that, seeing the foundling kneel
in the blood of faithful friend, to weep, pray, and seek
forgiveness for the wolf, repented, spent its life
shepherding the saint to all his wondrous works.
And Prince Llewellyn, returning from the hunt,
found his mastiff Gelert covered in gore.
Only after slaying the ever-devoted dog
did he find his infant son alive after all,
cooing near the carcass of a giant ravenous wolf.
Never was smile seen on Llewellyn's face again.

I wonder which is worse: living with a dead dog,
like Llewellyn, or a dead wolf, like holy Hervé?
There are no wolves in Wales today, finished by farm
and factory, city and chapel, though lots of dogs,
the streets slick with dog shit. No dangers now, just
a big, boring costume party, all of us sheep
in wolves' clothing with a bloody appetite
for the old sad stories.

The Others

Come away, O human child!
To the waters and the wild
With a faery, hand in hand …
                    —"The Stolen Child," W. B. Yeats

Did he climb this barren
height alone?
Lost on his way home
as twilight came
and went.
Searchers never thought
to look up here,
this terrible steep
where the only sounds
are the bawls of sheep
and the wind's sheepdog whistle.
Tommy Jones, five years old,
it says on the stone
that silhouettes this ridge
a thousand feet above his farm
and peers down into
the lonely lap of a faery
pool, bottomless, the locals say,
though its clear, green surface
shimmers, riffles, mirrors
whatever the changeling
shapes of wind and clouds
and light might want,
will have.

Two Minds

My mind is bad.
— Robert Lowell, "Skunk Hour"

I dreamed about her again
last night, forty years
ago back there in Georgia.
Here, in Wales, which the Gulf
Stream licks like a whelp,
ravens and gulls
hawk their hungers all day,
and gales shriek at night
like a cat fight.
Tides churn to clotted cream
on stones instead of scones,
and all the loveliness of yesterday
this morning aches and itches
like the hedgerows stitching
the fields, or like my scars,
still there, as if the good doctor
had sewn on new hands
but left the bad mind in.

Forensics

We go looking for Dylan
in Swansea, Dickens
in London, the Bröntes
in Haworth, haunting
the tombs and homes of the Dead
Proved Great.
Ghouls, stalkers,
paparazzi of the literati,
we can almost picture tiny Jane
herself, cloaked, hand struck
out to fend our cameras off,
as she dives into her coach and six
because she doesn't want her phiz
in *The Sun*, page three,
much less her knickers
splayed for all the world to see,
though as for sex, well,
Foucault already
stripped her right
down to the skivvies.
No wonder she hides under
the floor of Winchester Cathedral,
though we try to chivvy up the slate
and flash our bulbs beneath
that etched black door
to ogle the corpse that wrote
the corpus, the skull
that held the skill.

Fishing for Souls

I will make you fishers of men.
—Jesus

Van de Venne shows the two tribes—Protestants
aligned on the left bank, black-garbed
and bearded with those ruffled white collars—
Catholics on the right in scarlet robes.
In the waters between, their rowboats rescue
the damned who're sinking in sin.
It's a river, I think, like the Jordan painted
on the wall behind the baptistery
where I was dipped in a rubber robe at seven,
but these naked souls are drowning, flailing
and splashing. The recently saved
watch dripping from the shore
as the heretics, with their work ethic
and organizational skills,
have almost caught their limit, while
the Papists are nearly capsizing,
their bait the incense, music,
and gaudy dress that weighs them down,
and their nets, originally empty, hold
only souls the Dutchman daubed in later.
He's put himself on the winning side,
obvious from the healthy tree and sunlight,
amid stern elders like my father and
grandfather, who likewise fished for souls.
And though the other bank is clearly
in the wrong—evident by the lowering
clouds and withered tree—I like to think
the artist, perhaps just hoping for Puritan
patronage, took the longer view,

since the little man in the corner
looks out at us with an impish smile,
delighted by the struggles of
both rescued and rescuers,
and because the halves of rainbow,
rising from both banks and meant
to halo everything, run out
of canvas at the top and never meet,
but the river flows into a bay
extending to the horizon where
mountains part and let the eyes of all
of us pass upward and into
the distance, blue and buoyant.

Elect

Amsterdam, April 19, 2005

There's a rowboat out the window
that fills a little more each day
with showers in the afternoon
and the wake of cruising tourists.
We worry it will sink.

But today there is a bigger—
the biggest—fish to fry:
they're electing a pope, though
this most Protestant of cities is
unaffected and unimpressed.
The tall, narrow houses, high-
hatted as the big-bellied burghers
who owned them, continue
complacently leaning above
their reflections in canals.
The new burgers are also huge,
for fat Americans who seem to eat
in the same places, with our map
and guidebook napery.
It's sunny in Rome, but here the raindrops
pock the water and blur the glass
of our cruise-boat view of the trees
that are *leaving*, that pun the Jesuit
Hopkins couldn't resist.
And soon we, too, will be leaving
our room for Indonesian food,
another boon the Dutch brought back,
like the spices they traded religion for
and stuffed their warehouse cellars with.

As a famous American Anglo-
Catholic once said, April
is the cruelest month,
though today we wait for white
smoke and bells to ascend above
St. Peter's square like flocks of pigeons.
The devout would call them *doves*.
A new pope is being named while
the world is warming, and we're
still at war in a desert far away.
There've been two hundred and sixty four.
The two-hundred-and-sixty-fifth
will appear as if by magic
on every TV screen.
The little boat is green.

Roman Holiday

Over Frascati and olives on the sidewalk
of Bar Frattini, we watch the stylish crowds
pass by with their Gucci and Prada shopping bags:
beautiful young girls, slim in black,
olive-skinned and -eyed, and those distinctive,
tall, elegant, older men in perfectly
tailored, grey, pin-striped suits, silk ties,
razor-cut, silvery hair, patrician noses,
and shoes that cost a month's salary.

Then we walk past the Spanish Steps,
the Shelley-Keats house, the Trevi Fountain
to Edy for *insalata caprese*, prosciutto
and *melone*, tagliatelle with ricotta
and artichokes, grilled beef with *cippolini*,
and a good Chianti. We're at the apex
of our life, can't believe the odd offspring
of two dysfunctional middle-class
Southern families are walking arm-in-arm
along the Via Margutta past the very
apartment house in *Roman Holiday*,
the walls hidden in ivy that, in time,
will worm into the mortar and send
the house the way of the Coliseum,
the circles of a ruined hell.

And Peck and Hepburn, too, are long gone,
and we, back home, now stroke-
straitened, and crippled, learn all over

in rehab how to toddle, and then, as she says,
to graduate to mechanical straps and slings
of the Pinocchio prance,
then the walker and the Frankenstein stalk.

Is it possible those tall, thin young women
will ever age into the short, fat mama mias we saw
limping along, weighted with shopping bags,
or the smelly old crones bent to the ground,
muttering prayers, their cups out for coins,
or those elegant men shrink to the stooped
street sweepers early in the morning, when
that thick, dark coffee can be smelled
like the earth that warms, and wakes,
and raises us to our feet?

The Path to Iskeroon

They're all downhill from here,
the walks. The sun is up and so's
your energy—you could walk forever.
This is easy, you keep saying,
and everyone agrees and smiles
at how commandingly you lead:
Let's go even farther, the day's still beautiful,
as long as we're here, etcetera.
Sure, some rocks are slippery,
but you've got sturdy boots,
and even showers, great sky bruises,
leave rainbows when they pass.
Until you think that maybe you have
gone a bit too far (is that the tide
returning?); turning back, although
belatedly, might be a good idea.
Perhaps the map has lied:
its wee footpath of dotted lines,
like duck feet through the sand,
has vanished in the sea
that overtakes the strand, and evening
dims the green stained-glass
of country lanes. Oh dear,
and now there's rain again, but falling fast,
the way obscured, companions lost,
and what was easy at the start
has turned somehow so horribly
uphill, to slower steps that keep you
climbing deeper into the dark.

The Dead Use Us for Their Pleasure

My dead father led me to
Grand Isle, Louisiana, all
those dawns waist deep
in green Gulf water, fish
we never caught in Florida
when I was a child, jumping
onto my hook.

My grandfather wanted me
living in Wales, and Wordsworth
had to see me, a big fan,
sleeping at his home, Alfoxton,
even arranged it, celestial
travel agent.

Once, after my friend,
a great Hazlitt scholar, died
back home in America, he told
me in a dream to put roses
on Hazlitt's grave in the Soho
churchyard, and they burned
red as the tip of one
of his cigarettes
through the fog when I turned
to look one last time.

Portsmouth

From my window I can see the front
on this blue evening, where ferries
ferry to the Isle of Wight or set out

across the sea to France,
and the hovercraft hovers tourists
in circles of spray.

A big thing hoists people up and then
drops them, screaming, over and over,
down, and the rollercoaster and Tilt-A-Whirl

wheel like the gulls. The big, black, oak-tree
masts of H.M.S. *Victory* are hawsered
to the home of Gunwharf Quay after

whipping Napoleon. We must love
recurrence, there's so much of it we're willing
to pay for, like wars, marriages, and children,

the way we've kept coming back to England
for twenty-five years. I'd ask why, but
we all hate rhetorical questions,

or at least we say we do, the way we think
we're bored with our tedious life until it's
almost lost and we long to pat it again like a dull

car ready for another trip to work and back.
And what is a port, a key, or a mouth, anyway, but a way
to return to what we know and love, the fall

and whirl of the wheeling world,
else why not kiss just once
(goodbye) and leave for keeps?

Directions

There should be a long German word for it,
the way they string the little ones together
like Pullmans pulling out of the station of the breath:
The-Grieving-Leaving-Home-Feeling.
The Welsh *hiraeth* is for when you're far away,
but this is when you're homesick even before
you go, see the things and people around you
not in the glare of the now, nor in a rosy future,
but already in a golden past. Shakespeare and Stevens
had it right: we love most what we must lose.
And to those we leave, we say we have them *down*
in our address books, and they, to save themselves,
say they will look us *up* if they're ever passing through,
and then turn to what they have *left*, as if we
had already *left*, both of us *right*.

Our Lady of No Layovers

There are miracles all around us. A CD is a miracle.
—Joseph Campbell

A fortnight we've followed frescoes
across half of Italy, the Marys
outnumbering the Christs
three to one, the church giving
the pagans their earth mother to balance
in the scale the stern, sky father
of the Hebrews. Who'd have
the chutzpah to conjure
the face of the mother of God?
Yet, they did, and she has thousands,
all of them lovely,
and all different, as if each
artist imagined what would solve
his own loneliness.
Miracles color the walls: Jesus walks
on water, raises Lazarus; St. Francis
seals the blood inside the gaping wound,
reasons the ravening wolf
into veganism, pulls
a demon from the gullet of a maniac.

But we pray for the miracles
of the banal—that our plane's
on time, no sickness or toothache
to tax the halting languages
of clinics or casualty wards,
no scratch on the rental car, that

we get home alive in a coffin
of aluminum that flies
above the ocean and over
the frozen tonsure of the world.

Miracles
of the ordinary, like a plain
and small-town girl perched
on top of her drugstore stool,
flirting with the soda jerk
when the white-summer-suited
talent scout passes through
to see her sitting there,
and announces he'll make her "a star,"
take her to a place where people fly,
cull music from the air,
and watch a sheet like an unwound
shroud catch her face
and flicker it into forever.

O'Sisyphus Tours

One day of holiday
is very like another here
in Skibbereen or Schull:
roll from a mushy mattress
for greasy egg and limp bacon, soda bread,
a tube of blood-black organ meat
they call Clonakilty pudding,
then take another one-lane, bouncy,
dead-end, pot-holed road
along another peninsula
of heather, gorse,
sheepbones, and boulders.
Watch the Guinness foam of roughly
a thousand Atlantic breakers,
soaring seagulls holding on
against the gale, three dogs at the edge
of every village. Have some chowder
and a pint in a pub at end
of land, then track back
to where you started, the foot
of the buzzard-circled mountain
that reminds you what you left
and what you're going back to.

Holding on to the Pommel

These are the dog days, Fortunatus.
—W. H. Auden

From holiday we come home
to a heat wave, new fridge leaking
all over the floor, phone humming
a nasty little tune, lights that balk
no matter how many bulbs we try
till a blackout moots the point.
Sirius the dog star is ascendant,
but there's nothing serious about it,
no hunger or illness, only the imps
of perversity unleashed, given
free rein, as if God and the devil,
bored, on the job again, were betting
on the odd infidelity, argument, or sulky
silence, incapacities that short the wiring.
Nothing for it but to bring out candles
and like cowboys loosed from all
that is solid and still, try to hold on
till the horn blows, our brittle bones
all that separates what we thought
we owned from what we really do.

The Place You Belong

All your life you try to get back
somewhere, maybe the place
your family went on vacations,
where you always wanted
to live, cross the salt causeway
to see fish schooling, boiling
the aqua water, fishermen closing in.
Maybe Jesus dreamed in his tomb
of Bethlehem, always thought
he might get back, maybe even
retire—crazy old Herod dead,
and the sweet-faced wise men,
and the shepherds who let him hang
with them in the fields—
convert that little barn beneath
the date palms into something he could
live in, the desert hills in the distance
pink as his mother's cheeks.

Hounds of Heaven

Once, in Scotland, we stopped our car
to watch a man cull sheep from the steep
side of Ben Nevis. His whistles
to his border collie a mile away
scoured the stonebound pastures.
We staggered after his striding from hump
to hummock, small peak to peak—
his wild and white Jehovah hair, sky-blue coat
splayed behind him like a cape, tall crook in hand.
The slinking stalk and crouch of the dog corralled
the sheep that flowed from pen to pen
like salt in an hourglass.

Bible stories came back with them,
their stupid, black, Betty Boop lips
always working a gum of grass,
how they follow each other off cliffs,
stand bawling and lost only steps
from their mothers or the barn.

Now, we stop wherever there's a trial:
big green field, crowd of connoisseurs
in cricket hats on folding chairs, thermoses
of tea, binoculars tracking the streak
up the hill to do what the tweed-capped
farmer can't, though his shrill prayers
bring the dumb beasts, daft as humans,
down, through obstacles, around horrors,
to the house he holds open,
staff and arms outstretched
like the Good Shepherd himself.

I know one who runs to the door
as children leave for school, whirls
and whirls to keep them in.
They've brought wolves with them
through the eons, yellow, cat-slit eyes.

After, they're bathed in cool water,
happy to trot home
at the heels of muddy boots.

The Interpretation of Dreams

I was back in Georgia (where my Welsh
grandfather came to live),
driving an MG (all those driving tours
of England), going home
(Ohio), and found myself
in an underground garage (death), which I
tried to leave (live), but on the wrong
side of the road (England/Wales), when the toll
taker (my father) caught me. I knew
I could con him because
he was already weeping, saying,
"I was almost ready to leave
this country forever," and I
sympathized, and knew he would
tell me about his mother
(my wife) back home, who was sick,
and then he changed into a woman
with a beard (me), and then he let
me out with a golden token,
and I drove down the wrong way
into what happened next.

Twice Removed

France has been, as the guidebooks say,
enchanting, the Pyrenees frosted with snow,
and the food! Creamy sauces and snails.
But after a week, we're homesick, though
for America, where we live, or Wales,
where we're living this hopscotch year,
we don't know. *Home* is many-layered
as an onion, and none can make us weep
anymore. *Hiraeth*, the Welsh call that
inconsolable longing for place,
but we long for too many.
I like the way the plains Indians just
rolled up their houses and rode away,
took their few possessions and all
the people they knew with them.
What Mother couldn't move in a day,
the IRS got. What did they do, I wonder,
with my high school yearbook, all those
young faces stratified in the dark
of some warehouse somewhere?
If I could see even one of my graduating
class, I'd know how old I was,
but they're as scattered
as I. How do we put the heart
back in hearth? One *pied* in air,
we need another in some *terre*
besides the grave.

I still dream about my first house.
Now that was a home.
Where I fell on the floor furnace
that burned a chessboard on my knee.
Scarred and waiting for my next move,
look: it's still there, always will be.

III

STORM
SURGE

Persephone

When my wife woke from two months
of coma after a "massive" stroke with chances
of recovery "minimal," I sat by her
wheelchair in a class like a kindergarten
where kids of all ages cut colored cloth,
stacked blocks, and pieced puzzles,
and I wrote on a big pad in crayon,
"Let us go then you and I."
After she had read it aloud,
she went on in her whispery voice
to chant, eyes closed, the rest of the poem
from memory, while the rehab staff,
like the hominids in *2001: A Space Odyssey*,
gathered round and stood open-mouthed
as something odd and unintelligible,
yet somehow strangely familiar,
came to them from a far place, deep
and dark where she has been, beyond
the reach of light and love and words.

The Night Before We Left

It's sad how we paced from room
to room, our home already empty
without us, shrouded in our minds
like a summer house, all the things
we took for granted, damask
and down, the fired glaze of pottery,
glass, and gadgets. We left
at dawn to fly above the clouds, ice
crystals streaming over the wings, while
back at home already felt like
Pompeii before death flowed down
or sifted from the sky, our beds still warm
in the hollows of our shapes.

Cells

This is our new umbilicus,
like those childhood cans on a string.
Now, you're the baby we never had,
a preemie, struggling back
from your "fatal" stroke
to be my wife again. Our life,
for so many months, has been
nothing but machines.
They trace the lines that link
our fate like the stars of constellations
in a body recognizable
as whatever future we have left:
Orion the Hunter, Crab Nebulae,
Janus, Pisces, Cancer.

And now, another machine.
I hold it—little heart—always
in my palm, hoping to hear
the newborn life it might cry
from where you, silent, lie.

The Hard of Hearing

When my wife harassed me
to the hearing place, they sent me
home with a list of instructions
for her: "Call his name before speaking
to him," "Come into the room he's in."
She's outraged that now it's *her* problem,
and doesn't change. When I tell
my doctor, he says, "Wives
don't count—they've always
got their heads in a closet
two rooms away."
Now that she's
in a coma, I pray
real loud, intoning
help her help her all day
in case God has his head
in some closet two worlds away.

Long Love Sonnet

We felt anemic sometimes
among all the red-blooded
romances of younger friends,
and ours just the same
after all these years.
Now, as you lay in the hospital bed,
their passions, acetylene hot
at first, have grown cold,
and the seams they welded
groan, while our wedded love,
sick and old, banks in affliction,
still glows warm like embers
beneath our failing flesh,
our ashen hair.

The Angel in the Elevator

What angel, if I called out, would hear me?
And even if one of them impulsively embraced me,
I'd be crushed by its strength.
　　　　　　—Rilke (Gary Miranda, tr.)

They're everywhere,
not surprising since she's
in a Presbyterian rehab.
Pasted on every wall, they're
cute, though chubby, chiffoned, big-
butted, wings barely wide
as shoulder blades,
ascending somehow anyway.

And so,
I'm tempted to see them
hovering again, though
I can't seem to make myself
reach back to when, son
of a Southern Baptist preacher,
I believed.

And yet,
how can we bear
the miraculous without feeling
grateful to someone or some thing?
My wife, risen from a grave
of forty days and forty nights—
slugabed Lady Lazarus—
confounds doctors and Pharisees
on both sides of the sea.
Flying over the frozen pole, from

Swansea, to Cardiff, to Reykjavik,
to Goose Bay, Toronto, to Cleveland,
has any angel ever carried
so fragile a thing so far?
The floodwaters of her brain
recede, and the Lear Jet ark
sets down its cargo
with Technicolor rainbow,
in Youngstown, Ohio.

And so,
back on earth, we go,
reluctant but bold,
walking back, past
that doorman with the flaming sword,
into our first life
and reenter
our Eden.
I'm clutching her so tightly
to my side
she must feel
like one of my ribs,
as my fingers seek in *her* side
and hands for the healing wounds.

Smackdown

Sometimes I pray to God: okay,
if You want her that badly, take her,
end her suffering, mine too, relieve
those exhausted guardian angels
on duty so long their wings
have molted, their halos donuts
of flickering fluorescence
and insects.

But then I think, no, by God,
I'll wrestle like Jacob for her,
three fortunate falls out of five,
smite You hip and thigh
and other bones.
And don't try that cheap trick
You pulled on Lot—the only salt
will be what You sweat into
Your eyes before I kick You
in the cosmic nuts
and pin you like a butterfly.

But then You go and pull her, once
again, from her newest quicksand, her
Quick-and-Dead-Setting Concrete,
her imprint like an empty grave
to which I bring flowers to honor
what's missing. There are no atheists
in hospital waiting rooms,

only the mourning, morning visits
to the tomb, hoping for the stone
rolled away, and her not ascending
like dew-steam into some high heaven,
but coming back here, down into
the lowly embraceable body.

Praying

Pray without ceasing.
    —1 Thessalonians 5:17

My father being pastor of
a Baptist flock, our family prayed
without ceasing, although it sounded
to the neighbors just like yelling, bitching,
and carping. We couldn't stop jawing
with Jesus, who blessed our loaves
and tuna fish and haunted our hymns,
though I only heard his raspy answers
in wind through trees, the whining
of mosquitoes, and in surf
that gargled out its arguments.

Black sheep or renegade, I'm
no longer in the fold, though I
relentlessly recite before I lay
me down to sleep each night
that alphabet of dead or scattered names,
hunt them down in memory
as if I still could herd them all
through pearly gates, amaze St. Peter
ticking off his list of souls brought in
by prodigy, miracle even greater
than the tongues of Pentecost:
a wolf that learned the words
to shepherd home the lost.

Hutch

They always lived in tarpaper tin-roofed houses
out on lonely two-lane roads. My cigar-stubbed,
Coke-chugging uncle tried farming, then this,
then that, then rabbits. His sons
liked only songs about cars, played me
the records, "Little Deuce Coupe," "409,"
took me up to the tree house their father built,
and we rode a cable to the ground.
Then they showed me the little shack
out in the weeds, row on row,
tier on tier of mottled brown, black, and white
pink-eyed fluff and fur, pellets sprinkled
on yesterdays' newspapers. So lucky,
I thought, so many pets, honeysuckle
in the Easter air. Then he came,
opened a chicken wire door
and took one out, pinned it
by its ears to the clothesline
and pulled out his knife.
I hardly knew what I saw that day,
but like an afterimage of light,
a red disk burns in the dark
when I close my eyes.

St. David's Day

Remember? After breakfast of a proper
old greasy fry-up—eggs, bacon, sausages,
grilled tomatoes, fried bread, and baked beans
washed down with lashings of sweet milky chai—
we drove out to Rhossili,
an act of faith since it was dull
again, though the minute we got there
the clouds dissolved. We ate
pasties in a heathery little suntrap
on the cliff and looked at the Worm
while a farmer and three green-eyed,
black-and-white border collies
moved a bawling flock between fields.
Later, scones in a tea garden suspended
between the blues of sea and sky,
people down on the sands the size
of ants, and dogs running everywhere,
their tongues hanging out in happiness,
daffodils havering the leek-green Down.
In the evening, sex, sewin, and Gower
potatoes with Sicilian chard,
but American cherries big as apricots.
One of those days you want
to bottle, the two of us
the little figures under
a glass dome
atop a wedding cake.

Spot On

…some vicious mole of nature ….
—*Hamlet*

It's what the Brits say
when you hit the coffin nail
on the head, which this time
is another beauty mark
on her ivory back that has
imperialist ambitions.
Melanoma lilts like a lovely
spot for a holiday,
with a menu of chemo,
a bed-linen beach,
then the respirator's bubbling aqualung.

And we supposed I'd be the first
to go, with my hard-hearted
heart and liver-spotted liver.
I hate smart-ass Irony almost
as much as her pious stepsister
Sincerity, but now I'll wallow
in self-pity with the other pigs,
glut myself on punishment,
and keep coming back for seconds,
minutes, days, and years.

Three Stories

I hate the descent into the dark
of my cellar, all the things I failed,
felled by their own weight, old

golf clubs, tools rusting on a workbench
sprawled with spare parts, stacks of what
someone else's children will cash in

at the death sale, my pale spirit
sputtering protests at the paltry prices
inked on the tags, like the jug

we bought in Spain, sold for a song,
a dirge. Up in the attic, heaven
of dusty hopes, my former selves

have ascended to lie pressed
in the pages of albums, still fresh
in faded fashions, like a steamer

trunk of costumes that fit the ghostly
dressmaker dummies of young flesh.
And in the den, that treadmill

I supposed would take me
someplace new, a fast track to
anywhere but here, keeps me still

moving on the level in between.

Why We Never Had Kids

I don't know, except that indecisions
become decisions. We traveled
instead—France, Italy, Greece,
but mostly back to the same
old places, like Carreg Cennan,
"the most romantic castle in Wales"
that Turner painted in heroic,
sunset hues. Now, its ruin
is a rare-breed farm where
curly-horned Jacobs and spaniel-eared goats
crop the blood-soaked grass, the dry
moats full of wildflowers.

We'd drive an hour, climb
through suburban roads to reach
the single track that thrummed
over the cattle grid
onto the moor
and pull over, all silence and sheep,
sit there a long time in the tiny
bubble of buffeted rental car,
and look down on it, perched
on a cliff, aloof, alone,
impregnable.

Once, Driving in England, in Winter, in Rain

we stopped for lunch
at our favorite pub, bangers
and mash with real ale,
and sherry trifle. Later,
sated, on the drive back home,
suddenly the sun came out,
and my wife cried, "Oh,
pull over," and I did and looked
back over my right shoulder
at the valley burning bright green
and gilt. But, anxious to get home
before dark, I drove on again.
Why didn't I stop longer, since
this is my only life? Rain, and then
rainbows hooping the sky,
and the pot of gold of our little rental car.

Twm Siôn Cati's Cave

Before your stroke, and miraculous
recovery, our last hike (remember?)
was to find the legendary lair
of the bandit—a sort
of Welsh Zorro or Jesse James,
a hero of the people.
How we had to hold hands
as we stepped among the boulders
on the steep side of the gorge,
the cliffs opposite hooked
with the talons of red kites.
All around the hill we went
and never saw the cave.
Just as well, we say now,
since we were neither willing
to be robbed of anything
or enter any old darkness
before we were ready.

Tenebrae

*And when the sixth hour was come, there was a darkness
over the whole land until the ninth hour.... And at the
ninth hour Jesus cried, My God my God, why hast
thou forsaken me?*
                    —Mark 15: 33-3

Every Good Friday, I looked up
to see my mother weeping, my father
sure that by His lonely death

Jesus saves, that the darkness
was the sadness of God
swallowing the wafer of sun.

Half a century away, my mother mad,
my father forsaken, and both dead,
I pass the church announcing *tenebrae*

and feel the pull to stop and step
inside, snuff candles, douse
lamps until the light is gone,

taking all that it celebrates
and leaving me alone
with all that darkness saves.

Applesauce

That flattering tongue of yours that won me.
—*As You Like It*, Act IV, Scene I

Life is therapy, we say twenty times a day
and always laugh as she learns again
how to get out of bed, tie a shoe, lift
a spoon of rehab applesauce.
How much we took for granted, the little
mouse bones of the inner ear that carry
us over the bone-breaking earth,
the importance of gagging, eyes
that work in concert like a good marriage
or the voices of duet. But mostly
speech, that key that unlocks
the prison of self.

We wooed with our tongues
like Beatrice and Benedict.
Twenty-six years later, how many hours,
sun streaming into the white room,
have we struggled to be understood
with nods, blinks, mouth openings and pursings,
the frustration and tears, hands unable to move,
and how we wept the day she finally spoke,
no longer, as we like to say, at a loss
for words, so sweet in our mouths again.

Honey

Who was the very first to
broach the hive,
and taste it?
From afar, it must have looked
like only a golden drool.
Who found out the nectar
nestled behind so many stings?

It must have reminded him
of her, and therefore
he approached the unapproachable,
and suffered
to find this sweetness
that hurt so much
he returned again and again
to the tree that hummed
where four limbs came together.

Canterbury Tale

The flowers she buys at the grocery
spray from a jam jar, though we
can afford crystal now.
When in April, twenty years ago,
on the Tulane sidewalk, stopped
by a glance of sunlight on a bell tower,
she exclaimed, "How like this is
to Canterbury"—but pronounced it
canta-bree—I, Georgia cracker, frustrated
Anglo-, Italo-, Francophile,
was stunned, struck down by love, like
Dante by Beatrice, by her whiff
of cucumber sandwiches and tea cakes,
her skin like gold museum glint
on gesso, her legs of pink
Carrara marble, and her Jamesian claim
that American men were inferior
to European. So I scratched
my shaggy skull for foreign words,
took up opera, told her
I wrote poetry.

Turns out, she was from
Mississippi, and, Reader,
I married her—the salt lick
of her, the swish
of ceiling fans, afternoon
pinking the pillars of cloud
over the Gulf, gouache
of gumbo, pentimento
of peppery boiled crabs,
all washed down by
sweet tea in a jam jar.

Storm Surge

As the floodwaters of blood
receded in my wife's brain, the Gulf
engulfed the streets of her hometown.
How odd to be stranded across the sea
while watching on TV the stranded
on overpasses and in the ruptured Superdome.
Grand Isle, where we fished the surf,
nearly washed away, like the sands
beneath our feet in Wales.
What home could we go home to?
E-mail from high school classmates told
how parents and friends were safe, lost,
or still unheard from, though we knew exactly
where *we* were, Intensive Care, but at least
alive, not floating face down
in a bayou or back street. Bad
as it was, she woke up,
against the experts' odds,
and the city, too, proved tougher
than the pundits, already planning
another Mardi Gras, Papa Noelle,
Jazz Fest with its tubs of gumbo,
all of us rising to *fais do do*
into the future.

About the Author

William Greenway, a native of Georgia with a BA from Georgia State University and a PhD from Tulane University, is a professor of English at Youngstown State University. His poems have appeared in *American Poetry Review, Georgia Review, Poetry, Poetry Northwest, Prairie Schooner, Shenandoah,* and *Southern Review.* He has won the Helen and Laura Krout Memorial Poetry Award, the Larry Levis Editors' Prize from *Missouri Review,* the Open Voice Poetry Award from The Writer's Voice, and was 1994 Georgia Author of the Year. This is his ninth full-length collection.

About the Book

Everywhere at Once was designed and typeset by Amy Freels. The typeface, Optima, was designed by Hermann Zapf for the D. Stempel AG typefoundry and released in 1958.

Everywhere at Once was printed on 60-pound Glatfelter Natural and bound by Cushing-Malloy of Ann Arbor, Michigan.